ACTIVELY ACTIVE

ACTIVELY ACTIVE

This Adventure is a Joycean take on life.

Anthony P Prior

I, Anthony P. Prior, have written the book, 'Actively Active'.

To the best of my knowledge and in good faith, this is all my own original work of creative literature.

I expect my unique style to be respected forthwith.

Previous book, 'Stream of Consciousness' by Anthony P Prior.

FIRST EDITION

TONY PRIOR ART

978-1-80541-445-2 (paperback)
978-1-80541-446-9 (ebook)

CONTENTS

Anthony P Prior

Born Rugby 1958

BA Degree Fine Art Bristol 1979

Diploma in psychology & social behaviour
University of Warwick 2003

James Joyce Summer School
University College Dublin 1996

Built Enterprise racing dinghies.
180 in 18 years.

Married wife Julia, two sons,
One granddaughter.

INTRODUCTION

More of my style of lyrical anthologies essays,

Inspired to write about the ordinary,

As happenings as they happen or from memory,

Sometimes topical news or listening to the radio,

These affect my opinions and must document,

A busybody keeping busy for sanity,

Feeling apart of life's continuum continually,

Changing rearranging importance importantly,

An orderly order kept punctually as of now,

Prominent prominence proficiently pronounced,

Repetitively repeating concurrently conducive,

Correctly dissimulating arbitrarily defunct.

STANDARDS

I don't want to preach but these are expected,
Human behaviour varies from person to person,
The common factor common level generally understood,
What's expected how directed reflected decent decency,
Moral commonality of what we're used to,
Our ways shouldn't dominate flexible perpetuate,
Living together give and take friendly communicate,
Acknowledge both sides of difference.
Common sense commonplace no disgrace,
See who's obliged to compensate like or hate,
Differentiate differences opinions obligations,
Live together don't suffer stand up for common law,
Standards are set for working practices machines safety,
Old ways dismissed new inventory health and safety,
For our own good now understood safety's sake.
Budget in all costs when quoting for said job,
Part of party's party commonality understood for the good,
Acceptable acceptance expected expertly nothing less.

RIGHT FOOT

Get off to a good start,
Then everything else will follow,
It's true careful considerate,
Correct way to display,
Relieve all discrepancies,
Deficient malpractices,
Practice predominately,
Right and left look,
Cross over clear way,
Safety's sake to make,
All clear no fear,
Avoid accidents relent,
Positive commitment,
Belittle acquittal,
Got out of that deviation,
Started so I'll finish,
Happy accomplish,
Taken in reservation,
Law abiding jurisdiction,
Juries out no clout,
Left in no doubt,
Right away hear you say,

Compliant reliant,
Deft defiant,
Reliable circumstances,
Solid defences,
Recompense recompenses,
Arbitrary consideration,
Deferred obscured,
See clearly,
Deficient dearly,
Friendly Bentley,
Common decency,
Application applied for,
Had enough wanting more,
Stopped before start,
Got off on wrong foot,
Tripped over own feet.

RHYTHM TO PROCEED

I need music to start me off,
Kick starts my mind into thinking,
Then a list of jobs to pursue,
Order continues list persists,
Hastens my resolve to evolve,
Want to pursue in situ,
Change circumstances dances,
Can make wheelchair spin around,
And around play the dancing fool,
Until my heart's content repent,
Conciliatory bent lifting spirits,
Taking part being a part of important,
Not an "outsider,"
Want too frequently frequent,
Get with it relinquish,
In the groove improve,
Part of the party,
All moving along,
Metre sing song,
Bang a gong!

POSITIVELY INCLINED

Taking on an uphill challenge,
Irreversible procedure,
Leaving non-committals behind,
Interments terminal defendants,
For which relents arguments,
Argumentative to the core,
What's all the trouble for?
Whatever's maybe's let-downs,
Inclination direction subliminal,
Undercurrent of undeliverable,
Utterances spit it out drunken trout,
Don't pout now told off take it on the chin,
Think and begin again upwardly inclined,
Attitude divulge make sense not rude,
You tend to get misconstrued ideas,
Don't know where from filthy gutter,
You ought to work for that indescribable,
Newspaper gutter-press non the less,
Filthy pornography smutty indecency,
One look bribery mistook how could they?
Lives deficient in decency not proud,
Showing their way with all unscrupulously,

Certainly, turning the other cheek cheekily,
Morally indefensible beauty not cared for,
Hired photographed indecently pretentiously,
Negative downward slope inclined to fall,
Belittled downward slope slipping away,
Controversy argued argumentatively,
Awkward predicament predicts prevention,
Would be a better correlation making positive,
Strides do not deride deficiencies made up,
For wayward anthologies analytical differences,
Compliant with defiant disclosures not reliant,
On acceptable behaviour forth with detrimental,
Discouragements don't relent only get worse,
More perverse pedantic frantic wicked ways,
Driven by a haze of expectant glory,
Gloriously displayed purveyed harmoniously,
Portrayed with a portrait of a predacious,
Prominent purveyor seeking to gain favour,
With those in the know prominently,
Prospectively prodigiously promiscuously,
Lustfully forward advancing all guns blazing,
Not really comprehending said deficiencies,
Curtailing my advance uncorrelated procedure,
That hastens my nonelementary forth with,
Commissioned by a noncompliant benefactor,

Showing resilience to being downtrodden by,
Those not affiliated with the compliant alliance,
Venturing henceforth in to the unknown forthwith,
An undisclosed number of arbitrary chances,
That purvey idiosyncratically ideologically,
Surmounting opinionated opinions henceforth,
Not disclosing all parameters perchance,
Perambulating around the vicinity formally,
In a positive manner around the manor,
My patch manner couldn't be clearer,
Propose disclose prominent disclosures,
That prevail pertinently perversely,
Prodigiously unincumbered assertively,
Directly dissecting inadvertently prospecting,
Collecting collections commandeering adhering,
To vivacious lively personalities personalised,
Promiscuous personages philandering around,
Safe and sound going up next floor take it to the top,
Once more prodigious candid candour candidly.

PEACE AND QUIET

Set to work without radio on,
Distractions annulled cancelled,
Clear thoughts mind set,
Can think truly peacefully,
Ideas allowed space,
Making room dispel gloom,
Brighten up fresh concepts,
A good mood follows,
My writing amused,
Good state of mind kind,
I can write about anything now,
Don't get bogged down in highbrow,
Eyebrows lift persist,
Downplay hearsay,
Idle gossip controversy,
Don't listen to them,
Stirring up trouble,
Ignore on the double,
Everything is doable,
Troublemakers to one side,
Hide deride confide,
Talk about good to come,

Troublesome on the run,
Left behind right ploy,
Annoyed didicoy,
Devastate destroy,
Allow friends in,
Capitulate Serafin,
Serious command,
Bit risky alone,
Respect condone,
Put down frown,
Own devices,
Forward thinking,
Sinking feeling,
Navigate around,
Troubled waters,
Put down anchor,
Tie up fast,
Ropes from mast,
Contrast steadfast,
Holding trim,
Buoys buoyant,
Of course, reliant,
Calm before storm.

TIME SPENT PREPARE

Get things ready do or dare,
I care get right from the start,
Don't upset the apple cart be a part of,
A solid delivery commence recompense,
Misdemeanours are trivia trying not compiling,
Adding to problems denying forward progress,
Non the less countless risks calculated,
Loss venture capital capitalised upon,
Take the negative out of the equation,
A positive lead will succeed affirmative,
Delivery sets the pace no disgrace,
Race is now on to stretch out assert,
With alert confidence covert with,
Extrovert behaviour labour will work,
In our favour to build solid foundations,
From the ground up giving sound confidence,
To build up to the next level two stories high,
Brave telling stories about possible demise,
But can't happen as we have planned so well,
Contra indications indicative of overzealous,
Behaviour insolent of failure won't be entertained,
At this juncture due to confidence deceptive departure.

CHASING UP PREVIOUS

I must be on their records,
So, I'm trying to see if I still comply.
Not trying it on just seeing if I do,
It would be good to know if new versions,
Are available be good to be updated,
Hope by asking haven't created,
A new problem for myself,
New isn't always better,
Don't know unless I try,
Feel criminal or saint,
Relent argument,
Repent repentant,
Correlate delegate,
Commiserate trait,
Befriend friend,
Recommend pending,
Alleviate condescending,
Nothing ventured,
Nothing gained,
Set to remain,
Appease apologetic,
Be democratic.

JAZZ

Musicians play dizzily Dizzy Gillespie,
Saxophone breaks chords and silence,
Rasping high pitching squawking back down,
To base level rhyming chiming beginning again,
Pitching rising falling drawing away play,
Once more with collective candour,
All for screeching sectioning session,
Players all together now drink that,
Big black cow rhythm section same direction,
Elect to direct manifest gyrate complicate,
Smooth out break into harsh volume no room,
For nice tune sound chords must praise,
Me lord obscured chiming charming chimes,
Combine collectively rhythmically,
Obsessively mathematically duplicity,
Organically holistically binding,
Reminding of similar sounding sounds,
And of all that jazz buffeting belittling,
Harmony conscripting conscripts from,
Prison cells to merry hell as far as told,
Left to behold consoled beauty and beast.

OPERA FOR BREAKFAST

Highbrow nice change,
Rhythmical playful pirates of Penzance,
Pipes playing joyful tune,
Singing harmony rhyming,
Men's voices authority,
Projection proceeding proceedings,
Bold loud and clear for fear,
Far and near close,
Indigenous local accents,
Dramatic pedantic,
Romantic fanatic,
Assured positive,
Colloquial party,
Trumpets boost,
In time chime,
Woman's voice,
Highly charged,
Takes command,
Making a stand,
Delivering band,
Quivering vocals,
On the strand.

SIMPLE TASKS

Seem difficult and time consuming,
Got to get my head around doing the necessary,
Routine demands jobs to do,
See them off clear the way,
Obligatory hearsay says comply,
Obliged to reply to underwritten,
Morally conscripted afflicted,
Ascertained don't complain,
Get jobs done cross off list,
Before they persist awkwardly,
Perturbed reverb repeats,
Maintain regain without disdain,
Repetitive ordinary delusionary,
Press on contemplation,
Reserved for hopeful outcome,
About time for positive position,
Resolution resolves solves,
Forward progression conundrum,
Busy again happy with work,
Entertaining same but different,
Simple compliant defiant.

MOOD PROTRUDES

I must conclude I am moody blue,
Melancholy not far away,
That's to say affected by external,
Conditions sun rain restrictions,
Afflictions arbitrary imposed happenings,
Most of life is a battle to win over,
Have confidence to pursue,
Deluded protruded resume,
Defiant reliant compliant,
Overcome obstacles put up,
Self-imposed confused,
Mental blocks break down,
Suffer stop and go,
Delusionary should do,
Want could do can do,
If so, persist twist,
Out of ties lies,
Half-truths persist,
Strike off list,
Contest manifests,
Obligatory mood persists.

JUST SOLDIER ON

With my latest subscription,
Half-hearted conviction,
My jurisdiction is manifest,
Belongs to last conquest,
Behest done before,
I'll do it some more,
Encouraged encore,
Deplore same again,
To get in picture frame,
Sure, shot what I got,
Believe or not good delivery,
Considerate constabulary,
Official officer arrests,
Stood up arrested,
Contested contest,
Surely at my request,
To deliver fortunate,
Appraisal of luck,
Landing on my feet,
Not to deplete,
Boldly compete,
To win not retreat.

QUEENS SQUARE

There for appointment appointed a bit early,
Statute statue of Queen Charlotte prominent,
People parade past through across,
Lead by iPad messages read next stead,
Know where they're going ordered doing,
Cyclist pushes nobody rushes,
Calm broken by pounding pneumatic drill,
Shrill loud rhythm not still metal bores,
Jangle vibrate echo applauds job done,
Girls hand in hand masks hide smiles,
Pigeons strut around seat taken,
This vehicle is reversing repeating,
Conversation deliberating deliberately,
Converse rehearse stage play,
Last night's telly reencountered,
Pink trolley delivers busy on time,
Hammer thumps cell phone talks,
Blue scrubs doctor on call,
Nurses break time off allowed,
Crow bin in mess scavenged,
Unhinged glasses steam up,
Prominent tits stride bumptiously.

DEPENDING ON OTHER PEOPLE

Is difficult as self-made person,
I want to do everything myself,
To be sure of getting job right,
But have learnt to trust others,
Who will do just as well,
It's up to me to fully explain,
What is needed and expected,
Directed to direct with effect,
Working with people is an art,
Tactful explanatory ways apply,
Make it clear before disappears,
Hopefully enthusiasm carries on,
People picked up on my wake,
A way of showing applying,
Leading conceding default settings,
Appealing revealing consolatory,
Explanatory ways displays displayed,
Only one-way right way certainty,
Then somebody does it differently better,
Tried and tested manifests certainty,
Obligatory conciliatory concessions.

CHASING UP PREVIOUS

I must be on their records,
So, I'm trying to see if I still comply.
Not trying it on just seeing if I do,
It would be good to know if new versions,
Are available be good to be updated,
Hope by asking haven't created,
A new problem for myself,
New isn't always better,
Don't know unless I try,
Feel criminal or saint,
Relent argument,
Repent repentant,
Correlate delegate,
Commiserate trait,
Befriend friend,
Recommend pending,
Alleviate condescending,
Nothing ventured,
Nothing gained,
Set to remain,
Appease apologetic,
Be democratic.

CLEARING DROSS

The flat has been vacated leaving mess behind,
So, I had to ask Julian online to make fine,
He knew his worth and stuck to it,
More than I first thought told to,
Get with it live in the real world,
Consoled perpetual pervasive,
Petulant prominent persists,
To be struck off lists insists,
Amethyst shines stone valued,
Priceless commodity profundity,
What shines is gold all told,
Decent decency dismissed,
All for the sake of precious,
Commodity eyed up valued,
Could be nicked by persistent,
Fraudulent vagrant under cover,
Sister brother as one stone aplomb,
Don't realise the value its worth,
What on earth dearth devil's,
In the eye of beholder consoler.
Considerate jealous controller.

SOUNDS LOOKS

Even by email I can tell what she's like,
Her attitude was fair and forgiving,
Understanding cooperating nice,
Complying wanting to help pleasing,
Her manner was forthright doing,
Common decency appealing,
Sense of right and wrong,
Morally correct delectable,
Envisioning attractive personality,
Warm sensuality not long from,
Last calamity this should be better,
Correct to the letter of course,
Sensible rules apply forth with,
Embarrassed inconsequential partner,
Knows torment torrential terror,
Will make a drama if not appreciated,
Wants vows consequent sequence,
Who do we think she is?
Morally correct defect,
Decent decency detected,
Appreciative random beauty.

MAN WITH VAN

Being a landlord isn't easy having to put up,
With other people's problems excuses,
Dealing with tenant's abuse bullying,
Police being called also rent not paid,
Clearing out their dross when vacated,
Having to call and pay for Man with Van,
To clear out left behind rubbish mattress,
Acting as mummy to clean up after them,
Old smelly clothing shoes general abuse,
Left everything discarded as if retarded,
Never owned own home condone,
Furniture left behind Ikea was good idea,
Man with van had mate to lift nondescript,
Then head for tip landfill filling up in queue,
Recycling not being recycled a debacle,
Trivial had its day its use now in the fray,
Commissionaires commission commissioned,
Decommissioned no use anymore deplore,
Waste in a haste displaced loss of face,
Out of fashion in a fashion previously held,
Devilling compiling devilish description of,
Waste displaced commonplace today.

PROJECT PLAN

Getting things in order is crucial,
To make progress having a plan,
So, that I can ascertain correct way forward,
Also, a list of jobs to be ticked off,
So that time is not wasted haphazard,
An efficient progress of delivery,
An end goal realised promptly,
Items must be given space,
Find their own place naturally,
Objects demand where to be placed,
Ergonomically usefully pleasantly,
Let items talk respond to all,
Situations vacant jobs well done,
Project manager orders placements,
Best place recompensed capitulate,
Navigate delivery afore said,
To a home assertively,
Continuously progressively,
Assuredly architecturally,
Laid out in progressive format,
That can be read as a curriculum.

SUNSHINE REMIND

Bright not dull for a change,
Going to have to respond cheerily,
Just when I was accepting blue,
More to do feeling down,
Sun does put on a brighter haze,
Outlook good understood,
Must change rearrange,
Got everything to live for,
But still want on a plate,
Berate hate work jerk,
Perks not for me,
Solemn promise to chastise,
Remember still alive,
Same contrive,
Strict contradict,
Ideas askew,
Bent repent,
Help at hand,
Favours favourable,
Contrast ridicule,
Stupid boy play fool,
For a laugh,

Chess not draughts,
Thoughtful ways,
Along lines,
Up down across,
Diagonal take,
Known moves,
Game proves,
Misconstrued,
Advance,
Apologetic,
Romantic,
Quite a catch,
Befriend friends,
Make amends,
Ennui alludes,
Misconstrued,
Brighten up,
Coffee cup,
Hasten maker,
Genuine not faker,
To which this relates,
Harbinger of regrets.

KEEPING ACTIVE

Mind over matter is the answer,
Use it or lose it is true,
Push things to their limits,
Your body will respond to,
That's enough tiredness sets in,
Saying pause for breath,
Recharge barrage,
Listen to your body,
It will tell you when to stop,
Pushing these limits,
Requires fitness to achieve,
Doing more accumulates,
The body in good shape,
Responds eager for more,
The bar raises higher,
Mentally astute learning,
Challenging applying,
Defying ordinary,
Making extraordinary,
Adrenaline high,
Natural applies.

THE APPOINTMENT

Has been made but forgotten,
It wasn't at the front of my mind,
I was distracted time disappeared,
Got caught up in other trivia,
But this appointment was important,
I missed the call no sense of time,
Needed help to remind,
It's up to me complicitly completely,
Must not depend on other people,
Don't be an air head dreamer,
Easy to say after missing the call,
The connection dereliction of duty,
To myself misrepresented stealth,
Now to backtrack and reappoint,
Kicking myself gracefully forgiven,
This time forefront of mind be kind,
I'll make it belatedly forsaken,
More than just business pride,
Took myself for a ride,
Stupid boy controversy,
This time get it right be bright.

GET THINGS WORKING

Want to get the best out of what I've got,
Reassessing the use of objects and placement,
They might work better if rearranged,
More space given to ergonomically suit,
Surroundings let them breathe suitably,
Now more inclined to use them remembered,
Objects have a presence, presence of mind,
To be kind their use is more useful,
If placed correctly conveniently,
Aesthetically more pleasing to the eye,
They want to be used drawn in to play,
Satisfying collection recollection,
Of once used reborn in suite,
Items don't compete with others,
Happier placed with similar compare,
Sure to dare discover true place,
Where they don't encroach on others,
Object objectivity subjectively normally,
Correctly placed to perform subliminally,
So as not to trip collide ways around,
Soundly placed not done in haste thoughtful.

PLUMBER PLUMBING

Just getting one was a big job,
Terry a good one was all aplomb,
Conscientious simple jobs difficult,
Difficult ones easy all done,
Such a relief to have sensible,
Jobs fixed sensibly done not too,
Costly but now all working correctly,
Direct efficiency directly flowing well,
He's put a stop on inefficient radiator,
Replaced leaking stop tap,
Upstairs toilet now flushes,
Dual flush choice of,
Water softener realigned,
Choice of switch off points,
Whole house disabled from,
Kitchen upstairs bathroom,
Left on isolated conundrum,
Simply all sorted idiot proofed,
Ready to let clean deal appeal,
Got real seal deal demand high,
It should now fly to lucky punter.

OVERCOMING PROBLEMS

Must start the day with a clear mind,
Which means dealing with outstanding problems,
Some petty others important crucial,
Now I've tackled some as a matter of importance,
Less anxious and can now proceed,
Difficulties bothering harassing playing,
Contemplating avoiding unsolved revolved,
Coming back on me inscrutably has to be,
Discrimination poor relation to friendly family,
Self-inflicted pains remain unfortunately,
Jurisdiction causing minor calamity,
Good intentions still present problems,
Wish I could make people see originality,
Origin original at the time soon to be outdated,
Now contemplated navigated around said,
Difficulties forthwith without any problems,
Direct deficiencies directed away from,
A continuum curtailing correctly decidedly,
Pertaining to pervasive prominent assets,
Proving costly out of pocket persistently.

ESTRANGED

To lose the affection of someone previously friendly,
It does happen, people fall out with each other,
We all have particular ways ascertained to,
How we grew up got used to normal,
Most ways we share in societies format,
Well mannered respectful of space grace,
Good natured notice of intent relent,
Some over officious impertinent,
Look for arguments beg to differ,
For the sake of being different,
Their way is best conflict persists,
Made lists persistently begrudgingly,
Assuredly correctly in their eyes,
Funny tastes laughable pedantic,
Dramatic traumatic pathetic,
If only to resolve dissolved,
Dissipate can't relate permeate,
Congregate correlates diplomatic,
To a party of similar dissimilar folk,
No laughing matter strange joke,
Bespoke arrangements adhere to,
Conglomerates of apparitions,

Come to mind of similar kind,
Roles reversed well-rehearsed,
Needing a nurse to comfort,
Comfortably considerately,
Affectionately affecting,
Effortlessly effects to,
Dissimilate differences,
Between all parties involved,
Out of favour resolved,
Consoled console,
Game measured,
By way of credits,
Ascertained to victor,
Victoriously won over,
As the winner,
Not a beginner,
Make things trimmer,
With a tremor,
Only cost a tenner,
Cost effective my directive,
Don't have to apologise,
Careful of demise,
Build up again,
Out of picture frame,
Different not the same,

Can't complain,
Do it all again,
In reverse this time,
Alternate delegate,
Capitulate consolidate,
Navigate new terrain,
Same but different,
New view,
Interesting refreshed,
Different conquest,
Manifest bequest,
Behold bold,
Cajoled all told,
Consoled consider,
Considerate mandate,
Make changes,
To binding rules,
Only for fools,
Kept in line,
Once upon a time,
Life was fine,
Now it's complicated,
Needing to segregate,
Trivial to demonstrate,
Exactly what I mean,

Which averages out,
Keeping clean,
Distractions in-between,
Derisory compromise,
Friends still friendly,
After rudely abandoning,
Their hospitality,
Hospital nurse diverse,
Curses under her breath,
For what it's worth,
Inconsiderate dearth,
Apologising costing,
The earth spent up,
All commodities accommodated,
For more or less,
Balanced the books,
Solvent not crooks,
Straight dice contrite,
Wayward once or twice,
Belligerent complicit,
Dei-facto facsimile,
Factored into the equation,
Surmises sermon's,
To be read out to the,
Conciliatory congregation,

With the afore mentioned,
Derogatory sensibilities,
Of an immobile imbecilic,
Juvenile mentioned afore,
The correlation between,
The two said parties,
Was defamatory causing,
An inflammatory response,
Impatiently nurse's patient,
Responding hither to afore said,
Made better being left alone,
Placebo effect directly responds,
Strangely estranged recommends,
Albeit non comprehend allusively,
Names from personal directory,
They were friendly then why not now,
Drifted apart differences in art,
Tastes are subjective personal,
Don't like hate grate berate,
Consecrated grounds sounds,
Keep perspective within reach,
Narrow down common ground,
Similar dissimilar far-fetched,
But still within reach preach,
Suckers leach out badness,

Happy sadness barometer,
On considerate behaviour,
Which from my heart deliver,
A sense of fortuitousness that,
I can't deceive honestly leave,
My conscience won't allow,
Derogatory concepts of,
Self-gratification symbolising,
Wrong numeration of times,
Conscience reminds left behind,
Pricks my mind obey moral rules,
Of sense and sensibility conveniently,
For the sake of sanity plausibility,
Not disrupting correlating,
With estranged compatriots,
Friends who deserve treating well,
Not putting down condescend,
They are playing their part,
So, don't break their hearts,
Be convivial to lost withal,
Keep parameters within reach,
Don't preach they'll listen,
To common sense recompense,
Is my defence to overzealous,
Forthright decency descending,

Not correlating to concepts of,
Being amenable without quibble,
Sailing with an unassailable lead,
Fortunate forthright fortune,
Winning through all I can do,
Is set a standard for others to follow,
With the hope of good natured,
Contrariness doesn't reciprocate,
In derogatory condescending,
Putting in my place loss of face,
Lost the race tack about turn,
Ready about change sides,
Comply don't defy,
With all that gybe about who's right,
Play by the rules don't let fantasy,
Take control imaginary gestures,
Get the gist of collaborating with,
Other people's friends' recommendations,
Presenting different approaches to,
The same old same old problems,
Causing consternation constipation,
Stiff upper lip sees me through,
Commiserations to less fortunate,
At the races Harrogate in for a penny,
Loses ground several pounds,

By a nose compose dispose,
Left all behind follow in my wake,
Flare takes all without a fall,
Standing proud it is allowed,
Boots and braces wins at races,
Commandeer prize fortunate cup,
Polish silverware tarnish reputation,
Poor relation to victorious delegation,
With heads held high snobs snooty,
Winner takes home the booty looty,
Caput misrepresented presentation,
Awarded the prize don't deride,
My fortuitus ride first across line,
Winner takes all I recall,
Victory taken modestly,
Pays for the upkeep,
Unkempt if not victorious,
Pays its way commissioners,
Happy to accept direct,
With due effect payment pays,
Keeps ball rolling along,
Happy to sing songs,
Previously learnt nursery,
Rhymes help uplift,
Derisory benefactors,

Noncompliant with fortuitus,
Gains explained ascertained,
Making it worthwhile along,
Navigable waters sing,
Navy tunes gold doubloon,
Sea chanty aplenty,
Sung in tune rhyming,
Carefree not estranged.

DIGITAL NOT EMOTIONAL

Dealing with people affecting effected directed,
Takes good tact not to say wrong thing,
An art to approaching tactfully pleasing,
Presenting acceptable front paramount,
Understanding presented picture vital,
Showing concern adaptable flexible,
People aren't robots they're sensitive,
Humans need right directive constrictive,
To build positive relationship kinship,
Respond friendly in return please accept,
They can only come back reciprocate,
In a correct afore said constructive manner,
Building give and take relationship relations,
Emotional correlations friendly reoccur,
Now we can get on with the job at hand,
Without too much command demanding,
Not a robot a compatriot affiliated,
When we do get day to day robots,
They will have been programmed,
By us humans to be sensitive polite,
Maybe contrite considerate all right.

PROBLEM SHARED PROBLEM SOLVED

Problems kick up on a Monday morning,
I'll have to get someone in to fix the leak,
I've talked it through now know what to do,
Plumber will fit a new tap stop drip drop,
Leaked water will turn to ice not nice,
Prevent damage or a fall liable to all,
Everything linked repercussions forthwith,
Without doubt no doubt solve solution,
The only solution is to curtail run away,
Hearsays say's get it fixed clearly immediately,
To avoid swimming problem running drumming,
The right drip will only get worse perverse,
Consolidate stop permeate as of late,
Considerate consulate conclusion,
Bring an end to profusion delusion,
Water running away messy waste,
Causing misery to effected innocents,
Who don't need dousing in their housing,
Frantically stop the leak so not turn bleak,
Conciliatory gesture happy returns resolved,
Consoled done my best very best non-the-less.

ABSOLVED ABSOLUTION

Cancelled forgiven released from blame,
Guilt obligation forgiveness of sins,
Done wrong want to correct defect,
My dialect adheres me to familiarity,
Let off considerable calamity,
Don't do that again, promise,
Defect from the curriculum,
Current vein disdain,
Positively positive,
Can do better to the letter,
Confession relieves pressure,
Acknowledged wrongly foraged,
Give back not mine,
Borrowed for short time,
Absolute return learn,
Absolved sinner,
Hanging over,
Disturbed mind,
Clear way ahead,
Mighty dread,
Deliver peace,
Only fair release.

METICULOUS IMPETUOUS

I'm afraid to say this sums up my personality,
I am inpatient want everything yesterday,
In a precise order of delivery, a certain way,
That's my way of doing delivering merchandise,
Contrive in a rush hurry conspiracy afflicted,
Man know thy self I do this is true,
Age has made me slow down a bit,
A perfectionist perfecting peculiarity,
Attention to detail inherent afore said,
Done on time allowing for my confine,
A way of working quickly functionality,
Conscripted depicted plausible laudable,
Done on time remind sublime to an end,
Reputation depends on sound delivery,
Subsidiary of good upbringing homely,
Don't condone left alone thoughtful,
Do my best put to test impertinent,
Prescribed deride can't hide from,
Officious official impetuous meticulously.

IMPOSTER SYNDROME

Don't feel worthy or qualified,
To take on and tackle such afore said,
Out of my depth swimming,
Couldn't spell for a toffee,
Now know that isn't important,
With spell checkers correctors,
It put me off furthering a career,
Wish I'd had more confidence to pursue,
Study English at university,
Come to me later in life strife,
It all seems about confidence,
Recompense arrogance pretence,
Boldly head on anything presuming,
Trickster risk taker self-assured,
Conman salesman carry can,
No good carrying it off,
Getting away with it,
Must admit a trick,
Trick of the light,
Making it alright,
Fight or flight.

KNOWING LOOKS

Watching films looking at actor's ways,
A lot seems to be said with a look,
Of concern acknowledgement,
Expressing approval rejection,
Can be said without saying,
The obvious glance dismay,
Offering appropriate mood conclude,
Apparent abandonment love,
Joining dove's pairs affairs,
Warmth disapproval abandoned,
Close encounter joining together,
Falling out back together forever,
Reading letter sent spent,
Romance trance diligence,
Occupancy occupied denied,
Contrived seen done before,
Wanting more to applaud poor,
Dishevelled levelled all told,
Impressive bold catch hook,
Take another look as seen,
Embellished polished,
Performed well sold told,

Story straight navigate,
Narration followed,
Cajoled accepted,
Directed correctly,
Ineffectively direct,
Imperfect humorous,
Detect neglect,
Rest assured,
Improve mature,
All done for,
Effervescent shine,
Star sublime,
Reminded confirm,
Plot evolves,
Surprise told,
Lost move,
Downbeat heartbeat,
In retreat consoled,
Happy ending,
Want to applaud,
Of own accord,
Marriage in heaven.

ABOUT TIME

Things are expected to come about,
As a matter of order routine,
Expected delivery on time,
Setup executed each semester,
Taken care of not short,
Order of play no delay,
Time ordered manner,
Direct debit account,
Gets paid automatically,
Less virtual contact the better,
Don't bother sending letter,
No pitter-patter,
On time reminds,
Function functionality,
Punctual delivery,
Late delegates,
Library ticket expires,
Return items,
Back cash back
Cash in,
Insolvent returns,
Accountant alarmed,

Doing no harm,
Time to abandon,
Sinking ship,
Life rafts,
Head up,
Above water,
Sinking feeling,
Watered down,
Cork debulk,
Life ring,
Swimming,
Lifeboat,
Kept afloat,
Lifesaver,
Ship to shore,
SoS alarm,
Tapped out,
Dot dash dot,
All I got,
Brought ashore,
Rig commodore,
Saved life at sea.
Camaraderie.

APPRECIATED FREEDOM

Given a free hand at an early age,
Set me on a can-do attitude from the start,
Able to go to the Rec to play football,
Organise visiting friends after school,
Went for walks in open countryside,
Certain rules respect people's space,
Don't scrump gardens orchards,
Word on the street gained from friends,
Who to avoid keep clear from,
Gain remain pertain knowledge,
Where to go what to do friendly attitude,
I found cows didn't like my dog companion,
Saw him as a threat ushered out of the field,
Footpaths shortcuts bridleways lanes hills,
Along canals bridges rivers styles crossed,
Lay lines train lines roads farm mud hey,
Dogs protecting territory shut the gate,
Barking harking back discriminatory,
Exploring trails through farms skirt around,
Sweet smells silage manure steaming piles,
Walk for miles trials clean washing banishing.
Noses clean away from obscene keep free,

Derogatory conciliary councillor surveys,
Observing mess how people live impersonal,
Pride exhibiting values cars clipped private,
Privet hedge their bets doing up for less,
Countless number of tribulations malformed,
Abbreviated economically cheap hashed,
Quashed converted hidden perverted,
In a word absurd bittersweet lemon curd,
Brash hashed together done for now,
Hides big black cow presides over barn,
Doing no harm old infirm codger dodger,
Want to do better to the letter implicate,
Others ask for help pay the rotter,
Self-employed know better,
My accountant issues fair deal,
Pay income tax only fair compare,
Play a part in society notoriety,
Benefits from benefits beneficial,
Beneficially benefitting predisposed,
With wind on the nose self-disposed,
Can go anywhere having been diagnosed,
Freedom appreciated no other way I say.

OPTIMISM BIAS

Always looking on the Brightside,
Optimistic hopeful that things will improve,
Standing up against dull down mood,
Must be strong don't get misconstrued,
Fighting the devil dragging me down frown,
This dissolution born of confusion,
The solution is to not be daunted,
Chin up, hold head high to defy,
Think of things to make life easier,
Problems persist against conversationist,
Make a list of jobs outstanding reprimanding,
Financial problems persist top of list,
Deal with those first resolve cajole,
Ways around Stoney ground compound,
Dishevelled shovel mixing setting concrete,
All around my feet can't delete complete,
Annoyance try avoidance coincidence,
It's happened before such a bore,
Should know better a competitor,
Always striving not arriving,
Result a poor result at last,
Optimistic ballistic cataclysmic.

DON'T LOSE FLAIR

It is what keeps me going,
Have confidence in yourself,
Got used to same old same old,
Won't be told let life unfold,
Must push the river to deliver,
Forthright without quiver,
Know what to do must do,
Trusting in my conscience,
An automatic response,
Unravel drivel from conceptual,
Wrapped up in idea to pursue,
Thought it good now not sure,
Be realistic out of my depth,
Want the impossible, rejected,
Neglected plausible outcome,
Fantasy wanting dreamer,
Stream come clean,
Often thought about,
Without realising,
Probably could happen,
Commitment harassing,
Left me convalescing.

CUT IT OUT

Leave it out,
Forget it,
You're joking,
No way sunshine,
Better alone,
Stop the rot,
Get help,
Call the police,
Leave alone,
Don't condone,
Black spot,
Around the bend,
Make amends,
Trivial pursuit,
Be cute,
Greedy slob,
Big snob,
For the richer,
Poor man's apron,
Dishevelled levelled,
Corny joke,
Seen better.

BIG CHICKEN

I was aware of the pecking order,
The big chicken was moderately placed,
His big bold build suggested bravado,
Submissive effeminate showed sensitivity,
Delicately applied to butch job certainty,
Carried it off professionally done,
Equal to the job certainly correct,
Daintily direct didicoy ploy,
Small and large contradict,
Powerful cement mortar,
Applied to next block of bricks,
Skilfully rendered render,
Done in a trice always nice,
Trowelled correct amount of,
Mortar to brick ends next laid,
Upward stroke to squeezed spoil,
Efficient mix determinately,
Confidently succinctly delivered,
Revaluating first impression,
That satisfied delivered assertion.
Full recommendation ascertained.

WHAT'S HAPPENED TO SOCIETY?

We are in a state of stagnation recession,
Depressed economic rampant inflation,
Trouble putting food on the table,
Government indecisive not inclusive,
People are harking back to 1970's,
Punk revolution dissolution dissolving,
Old music of the times back in fashion,
Making the old feel younger I remember,
The bad old days glam rock Gary Glitter,
Sad pitter your wits to survive alive,
Shops being boarded up frail sales,
Unemployment redundancies apprenticeships,
Apprentices tattoo and nail parlour's apparent,
Coffee shops rent arrears area's differential,
Differences disappearance's dissolute,
Lost control of absolute forgiveness,
A steal dead giveaway commissary,
Commissioned no intension of paying,
Credit where credit due compliant,
Not reliant death defiant subversive,
Tendencies curbs coefficient collaborations.
Winter of discontent not obedient disobey.

KEEP WORKING

Keep on keeping on currently correctly considerably,
Considerately conducive of consideration to all,
Involved in working towards a fortuitus goal,
Never thought I would put away the winner!
If you don't try, how will you successfully succeed,
I've tried to acknowledge what's needed,
When seen a problem done my best to fix it,
If been unable got someone else to do so,
It's difficult to accept, I'm used to doing,
Everything myself Mr independent self-reliant,
Compliant duty doing the necessary,
Not defying skiving taking the easy way out,
Work is the food of life compliant jobs to do,
Routine demands what next when perplexed,
Vexed context to be written about in script,
That depicts definite order of doing a list,
Done before contrived derived implied,
What should be done diddle-Dum conundrum,
Leave it out sing and shout ordinary enjoyable,
Work doable affordable one accord plays.

RESPOND TO PRESSURE

Sometimes it's good to be pressured,
Heightens your awareness and assertiveness,
But must be aware of overreacting,
Pressure can open a whole new can of worms,
A forced issue reassesses the afore said problem,
In a new picture frame picturing pictured picture,
In a new light presenting presence of mind,
Obliquely obliterating obstructions obscuring,
By definition obstinate little obstacles blocking,
The afore said obstruction stopping a clean flush,
A good hand floater ace clearing the way,
Hence forth not allowing the joker to bypass,
By all means adventure adventures advantageous,
Discriminating discrimination obliteration obliterating,
A numeration of algebraic incarceration's numbering,
To a full calculus displaying an indenture invented,
To preclude rude brazen mistresses demanding,
That they should be heard not herded along,
Like a flock of sheep to be marketed at market,
To the highest bidder auctioned off bidding,
In a hypnotic rhythmic response sold on high.

LONELINESS

I always make myself busy,
Not rushed pushed for time,
I organise have a routine,
Not enough hours in the day,
Openly make a display,
Commissionaire's commission,
Get involved with people,
Talk chat come back,
Doing rueing moving on,
A lot to be thankful for,
Why is life such a bore?
Has it all got repetitive,
The same thing over and over,
Something's bothering me,
Not sure what, all I got,
Thickens the plot,
Got things to look forward to,
Still, I rue what I want to do,
Sometimes tricky,
Made problems for myself,
All alone self, below par.

SPARROWS

I am Jack sparrow,
Brought up as a family in a nest,
It's been a squabble,
Between my sister's and me,
Fighting for space,
In the race to grow,
Parents keep us warm,
Body heat sat on,
Food is delivered in turn,
Scrap yearn,
Cold out,
Head down,
Chirping,
Volume high,
Blackbird screech,
Out of reach,
Teach each other,
Lie low,
Hawk murder,
Take sister-brother,
Look after each other,
Calling out,

Chirping pout,
Noise protects,
Parents too,
Alarm call,
Soon fledge,
All huddle,
Gone tomorrow,
Team sparrow,
Brought up well,
Competition lichen,
Temporary home,
Nest contest,
Avoid predator,
Hawkish behaviour,
Parents have delivered,
Considerate considered,
Pest in nest,
Squirrel squirreling away,
Weasel theft,
Bereft nest,
Numbers at large,
Winners survive,
Sparrows alive.

RASPBERRY CANE

Today I woke as a growing raspberry shoot,
Hoping to grow tall and bear fruit,
My shoulders pushed through the soil,
My D.N.A leader firm and succulent,
That's translucent disseminating about,
Forcefully growing in upright motion,
I'm through head and shoulders,
Above ground safe and sound,
Breathe air going to be sumptuous fare,
Gardeners tender my tenders,
Tying me back to bamboo cane,
Which will support my rapid,
Rise fortuitously currently,
Predominantly be the bearer,
Of delicious fruit in demand,
Well looked after fed and watered,
Regularly picked and clipped,
Fence with mesh adorned,
Lovely mulch aphrodisiac,
Put on a spurt to impress,
Countless birds' trespass,
Plunder my bearing fruits,

Steal my wears they dare,
Not fair gardeners fare,
If you don't like it I will,
Blow a raspberry up yours,
No decorum attitude problem,
Fight for survival convivial,
Don't mind if birds take,
They will spread pips,
I could spring up anywhere,
In the spring advancing,
Spring in my stride,
Don't deride confide,
Spread the word,
Beautiful fruit to collect,
Far and wide dialect,
Not fussy anybody,
Blousy boozy bumptious,
Causing rumpus,
Fight over me,
To be desired,
Only natural conspired,
Flirty androgynous delight.

BLIZZARD

Today I am holistic the sum of many parts,
Flakes blistering bamboozling accumulating,
In a rush falling blown along,
The storm has created me,
A mass of flakes tumbling,
Rolling as tumbleweed drifting,
In a desert deserted road,
Defined by tracks made,
Cactus trees project,
Out of sand snow clinging,
Horse hoof prints followed,
Tied to a coral stabled,
Straw leads to stable,
Harness harnessed,
Bridle tied lashed,
Around compound,
Swirl of flakes,
Whirlwind travels,
Swept along,
Buffeting buffers,
Bouncing colliding,
Collecting momentum,

Rolling over forming,
A snow dust bowl,
Tumbled over and over,
The wild rover,
A ball of flakes,
Visually dizzy,
Complicit illicit,
Wouldn't normally,
Be here for fear,
Of melting away,
Solid ball bound,
As one conundrum,
Rolling collecting,
Increasing exponentially,
Drifting along,
Sound of wind,
Whistling call,
Hinges of gates,
Ok coral,
Rider in saloon,
Whisky down.

THERE ARE THINGS ON MY MIND

Got lots of things bothering me,
Some really stupid obvious,
Countless times I've thought this,
We have an energy problem,
Shouldn't we be utilising twice a day tides,
I know it's been thought about,
But nothing happens,
Wildlife opposition disturbing habitats,
Tidal dams across estuaries,
Turbines generating power,
Wildlife would have to adapt,
If we make salmon runs,
Eel bypasses bird nesting sites,
Locks for boats to climb,
We put money into wrong projects,
Climate change is rearranging anyway,
Solar power and storage stop shortage,
Green energy blue turbines remind,
Lots of ideas to help wildlife,
The environment we all repent,
Must succeed stop the greed,
Be convivial long live revival.

PLANT RUNNING

To seed has usually finished flowering,
Done its job born fruit set seed dispersed,
Flower power attracted bees fertilised,
Grow on bear fruit conducive illusive,
Nonintrusive contusive say good delivery,
Commissary to losers of community,
Failing to communicate afore said delusionary,
Dissident delinquent disobeying derisory,
Disillusioned dissolution disabling decorum,
Forth with without due care declared as,
Intrusive retribution illuminating shining a light,
On bright objects of a cosmic nature illuminating,
Bright ideas as to how this all started with regard,
To a heavenly sighted star from afar distant,
Cousins bearing no relation to a cartesian well,
Well before a calamitous calamity engulfed,
The abridged cross-over into,
Enormous plant earth moving,
Ploughs up field making way,
For smaller JCBs to cut edges,
Smaller, neater completer,
Abridged version builds a bridge over,

To form a viaduct over disused land,
Taking traffic away bypassing established,
Village church houses farm buildings,
Tractors trailers all for moving equipment,
Manure to be spread fertilizing said,
On the land so plants can be sown,
Seed crops grassland for cattle,
Drainage taking excess away,
So as not to muddy field damage yield,
Carefully thought about old trout,
Experienced in matters of improving,
Advancing performance higher profit,
Business growth using my loaf to expand,
Pay good attention to green details,
Harnessing natural resources at hand,
Efficient wind blows blowing away,
Useless subsidiaries subversive tendencies,
Only deliver fractious commodities causing,
Derisory delusionary decorum in dissolute,
Disused establishments offering nothing,
To anybody at any time useless plant,
Dead in its pot all I got dead still on earth.

OWN DEVICES

Art college at first left me unsure insecure,
Then because I wouldn't listen to anybody,
Anyway, total freedom seemed natural to me,
Self-assured found my own space common-,
Place other students to own divide complied,
Our mission seemed to be share differences,
Lectures influenced process and attitudes,
Far afield experiences talked about reasoned,
Philosophical logic platonic intellectually,
Put into practice left to own devices advised,
Visiting artists sociologist's philosophers,
Made my course a kind of therapy to join,
We were all individuals trying exploring,
Copying seeking originating collaborating,
Going one better pushing further from,
Safe ground ideas paramount conceptual,
Freedom limits evolving changing asserting,
Deregulating confiscating forming aborting,
Taking from, making own choices devices,
Total freedom random achieving success.
Made better convalesce temptress taken,
Life changing revelations compilations made.

NON-SENSE RECOMPENSE

My Defence
Makes sense to me deliberately,
Want to assert myself positively,
Reckless days behind lost mind,
Logically do the right thing,
Not going to make a song and dance,
About new advance forward,
Boldly hence forth for it's worth,
Ignoring a depth of online propaganda,
Having a look for something else,
Know what it is when I find it,
Still searching lost and found,
Common ground all around,
Loud sound echoes rebounds,
Reverberates pronounced bass,
Thumping shakes foundations,
Loose items fall from grace,
Loss of face displace,
All that's commonplace,
In situ statue,
Statute north,
I declare worth,

Money well spent arrogant,
Those who repent,
To hearts content,
Confide misspent,
Reimburse lost out,
Painful shout no clout,
All about nowt,
Reimburse trout,
Caught by fly,
Senseless pry,
Catching awry,
Smiles defy,
While comply,
Do or die,
Pity small fry,
Bigger a trigger,
To start afresh,
Something new,
Not done before,
Difficult old reborn,
Different strategy,
Instil new life into old,
Fashionable appraisal,
Common decency,
Manners makes man,

Accepted clan,
Not a clique,
Bit oblique,
Try unique,
Different view,
Makes new,
Accepted true,
Aline confined,
To sublime,
Spirit based,
Dissolve waste,
Disappears haste,
Solid base,
To launch lunch,
Got a hunch,
Pretty bunch,
Flowers powers,
Colours attract,
Display packed,
With promises,
To be kept,
Little indirect,
My neglect,
Cause and effect,
Inspect evidence,

More recompense,
Always paying out,
In for a penny,
Compound pound,
Adds up to sound,
Investment multiplied,
Many times, over,
Playing wild rover,
Discovering bother,
Mother of troubles,
Russian Roubles,
Cash in hand,
We all depend,
World revolves,
Around our spend,
Depending on make,
Unselfish take,
Profiteering,
Capitalist pig,
Irish jig,
Confounds rigged,
Apportioned to,
Stupid idea,
Spent in areas,
Backward thoughts,

Not thought through,
Irritable solution,
Not fare conclusion,
Suffer delusion,
Protrusion stuck out,
Disembogued rude,
Get away with it,
Complicit deficit,
Fraud me Lord,
Connaught report,
Around little finger,
Let it linger,
Bringer buy sale,
Give and take,
Somebodies make,
Profits from fake,
Conned implicate,
Sucker's fools,
To fall for joke,
No rebuke,
Get back,
Lost ground,
Recover compound,
Secluded diffused,
Abused refused,

Intrudes confused,
Simpleton guilty,
Of taking lion share,
Compared to dare,
Lucky side deride,
Confide hide,
From embarrassed,
Situation no relation,
To poor navigation,
Taken wrong turn,
Which learned as,
Sell going concern,
Profiteering going well,
Away from merry hell,
Dispels tell tales.

LYRICAL LANGUAGE

Defines writing for me,
Something I identify with,
Rings true can do,
Maybe contrived derived,
Ended up poetic lyrics,
Try to avoid conflicts,
Words depict visions,
Descriptive lessons,
Experiences learnt,
Experienced expert,
Extroverted exert,
Exerted exception,
Looking for redemption,
Repudiated reputation,
Ancillary exile,
Definitive definition,
Argumentative coalition,
Cohabiting condition,
Sharing pairing,
Nice pair with flair,
Aux contraire ordinaire.
Plain and simple,

Missed chances deplorable,
Can't afford not to,
No going back flack,
Get own back,
Have in a way anyway,
Considerate illiterate,
Spell it out caught out,
Drunken fish trout,
Drowned sorrows,
From whom borrows,
Street narrows,
Afflicted conflict,
Make peace police,
Contravene laws,
Indenture deplores,
Caught red handed,
Guilty as hell,
As far as I can tell,
Mission to deceive,
Takes more than needs,
Greedy so and so,
Deplorable fatso.

CHANGING IDEAS

Solving problems can be easier than first thought,
Disappointed but might be better rearranged,
Bringing on different ideas being adaptable,
Flexible commendable responsible deferred,
Conquered absurd not possible ridiculed,
The difference deferred different does,
Brought about many changes suiting parties,
Appeasing reluctant assertive rules ruling,
Could have fooled me protraction protracted,
Predominately persecuting inflexible triers,
Reliefs of persistent prevalent persists,
Now struck off lists ascertained predominately,
Deferred with regularity persistently prevaricating,
All around the problem producing protracted,
Assailants forthwith hither to forth perambulating,
In a perturbed manner prescribing medication,
To cure the incumbered number of persistent,
Petulant insolent innocents insolently diverging,
To avoid detection as a guilty party resolved,
In full retribution relocated divergent diverged.

POSITIVE INPUT

Came from having a good night's sleep,
Refreshed blessed not under duress,
Often feel harassed first thing,
I feel lighter brighter sun shines,
Thinking sublime not confined,
Reminded previous actions able to,
Do more of the same again easy now,
It's not repetitive fresh outlook to book,
Not going to be misunderstood,
Clear as a bell rings true must do,
A weight lifted uncomplicated assertive,
Positive input brings about new true,
What I must do can do will do true blue,
Confessional character appraisal,
Appraising liaising comforting comfort,
Comfortably singularity duality apart,
Leaving a senseless start sensibly,
Contradicting contrived derived,
Positively punctual on time reminds,
Assertive directive directing directly.

RETURN TO ARTWORK

Had a consolatory moment felt lonely what should I do?
Troubled mind felt confined only one thing to do true,
Alleviate by navigate pencil to paper draw,
Scribbled randomly abstractly deviating from,
Representation to corelating a form of form,
Lines resemble a face highlighted feature,
Prominent a nose chin caricatured as if,
The bard Shakespeare himself left on the shelf,
Dishevelled seen better days globe of ideas,
Theatrical experimental reminiscent of playing,
A jesters joke on stage to an audience about,
To be auditioned for Hamlet, The Tempest,
Stage set for play on words absurd deferred,
Conquered satirical no laughing matter quizzical,
Jesting the actors to play jester, conquering,
Blackadder recanting rehearsed pronunciation,
Equivocal bilingual times once past old days,
Return to old ways of painting displays,
Styles impressions expressions modernist.

BLA-DE-BLA

My personal colloquial summing up of situation,
My wife would know exactly what I'm talking about,
By the tone of my voice and direction it's aimed,
She couldn't agree more backing me to the hilt,
Even if my lilt is full of slander she understands,
Swearing topical news translated with a bloody,
The Bla-de-Blas had it coming to them!
If they can't be more decent, they'll get it
They took me by surprise lazy deride,
Followed by my derogatory Bla-Bla not conciliatory,
About been left alone consolatory confined,
It's times like these I need to clearly appease,
I can't always put wrongs to right but,
Putting the Bla-Blas straight to tolerate,
Is positive navigate deviating from hate,
A trait to contemplate complicit alleviate,
Sad state of affairs always dares Bla-De-Blas.
Common decency feeling nonentity.

PEDANTIC PLANNERS

Set out rules of how I should behave,
Treated as an impassive embroiled imbecile,
They're in charge know the rules stop all fools,
Who are bound to be trying it on getting away,
With it complicit fraudulent dodgy builders,
Who are in it for the money irresponsible,
Their job is to check double check refuse,
Can't be reasoned with insolent boy go away,
Ones who have got away with it corrupt complicit,
Only doing their job set rules standard remanded,
Bypass Parish council first good church rehearsed,
Conversed convalesced concealed revealed,
I feel branded reprimanded cowboy blazing,
I've tried rephrasing spelling it out but nowt,
Lost all clout emblazoned reasoned shopped,
Known criminal activity realised defiled,
Just tried to bend the rules a little,
Cough and spittle until acquittal,
Seemed only fair that I dare,
Not so now I know from below.

BREAKING RULES

Given a rule book at school to follow,
Told I would break them prefects would punish,
Lived in fear of indoctrination poor relation,
Navigate around the safe and sound,
Put into detention no affiliation comprehension,
What have I done cheeky face disgrace,
Have to write lines many times,
Inhospitable until acquittal let off,
Disgraced face humility pity often,
Bearing no regard to senseless sense,
Safe sitting on fence augments,
Which side are you on conundrum,
Turned into good laugh giraffe,
Sticking my neck out obscene,
Gesture gesticulated confiscated,
Berated over and over controller,
Harbouring ship to shore ignored,
Don't know what for candour,
Ridiculed some more deplore,
Rules for fools disembodied.

INTUITIVE GUESS

I guess I calculated this might happen,
And it did an opportunity had to be taken,
A carrot dangled in front of my nose,
A gift opportunity I didn't really want,
A golden opportunity benefiting "Moi",
Stupid not to take be a part of,
I had surmised a collective happening,
Dead reconning positioning position,
Have since thought it through now,
Knowing what to do simplistic can-do,
By taking part shows interest must persist,
Don't really know where this is heading,
I've read about similar opportunities pending,
The chance seems a long shot tempting,
If it comes off, I'd be profiting concluding,
No illusion or delusion confusion protrusion,
Got to stick it out to benefit from chance,
Diligence equivalent sequence,
Sequential to follow correct line profiteering.

GO UNDER THE GUISE

Disguises apologise no compromise,
Harmonise individual hiding surmise,
Keep alive promise to survive,
Fortuitous continual drive,
Subliminal self-stay alive,
Guiding driving contriving,
Done it before do more,
Absolutely resolutely,
New year's resolution,
Born out of confusion,
Promise to improve,
Get in the groove,
Excuses elusive,
Conducive concur,
Arguments defer,
Ignore smear,
Brought down,
Joker clown,
Frowns alleviate,
Lot to contemplate,
As of late deviate.

DIFFERENT OPINIONS

Must be listened to appreciate accepted,
Its variety variations are creative productions,
Allowing for new ways of thinking doing,
A different direction way of looking at old,
Established static circumstances same old,
Unimaginative interpretations seen before,
Old fashioned modernist equilibriums,
Set in stone don't condone being prone,
To repetitive directive not selective,
Appreciating variations eliminating,
Same old same old ways that unfold,
Nothing new inverted perverted,
Discriminated assimilated perversions,
That rot the mind not kind of anybody,
Assailant's deviants of normal
Moral standard persuasions,
Persistent prevailing profusely,
Tantamount to disastrous regulations,
Regulating afore said distributions,
Discouraged by simple simpletons,
With no flare don't even dare to care.

FORCED CHANGES

Having to adapt brings on new ways,
Thinking around a problem changing,
Realising there are other ways of doing,
Firstly, looking at resources at hand,
Finding another use at my command,
Brings about adaptive recollective,
Resources are good reused,
Make them steady steadier,
Transforms their use,
Helping me walk truly not wobbly,
Confident not going to fall,
Assertive directive collective,
Adaptive improve reconfigure,
Not left to chance well-balanced,
All things considered works,
Used to be straight forward,
Now confidently adapted recollected,
Use reconvened as seen confidence gained,
Kept plain realigned set true.

APPLYING THINKING

Got a job that needs doing,
It should be simple enough but tough,
Straight forward now analysed recorded,
Taken measurements up across width height,
Drawn a plan, surely I can get it right,
It's been a while life on trial,
Making is constructive productive,
Something I can do, definitely will,
My own project manager prospecting,
Know what to do set straight,
Too easy to delegate complicate,
Set square measurements tie in,
Diagonals right angles not meek oblique,
All figures solid structure conjecture,
Deliverance disappearance not problematic,
Getting head around job not fobbed off,
Assuredly conformity duality reality,
Pleasing reason formality formal,
Proud satisfying solving revolving,
It's all come true again can-do.

MEMORY

Is everybody's kingpin status of what we are,
It defines refreshes reminds not always kind,
Embarrassing situations we want to forget,
Linger harassing complicating deferring,
I said I wouldn't do that again but did,
Repeating let-down never learn yearn,
Same old same old same age not told,
It does add to experience done before,
Want some more, easier this time,
As well as next time perfecting ways,
Confidence displays ordinary similarity,
Naturally considerably confidential,
Privately reserved move on perturbed,
Held in respect different dialect detected,
Away from home dissimilar condone,
Knew putdown was coming bludgeoning,
Condescending remark said for a lark,
Funny for everybody at my expense,
No recompense or recompensed return,
Take it on the chin accept funny laugh,
Agree situation comedy ha-ha move on.

MEMORY

Is everybody's kingpin status of what we are,
It defines refreshes reminds not always kind,
Embarrassing situations we want to forget,
Linger harassing complicating deferring,
I said I wouldn't do that again but did,
Repeating let-down never learn yearn,
Same old same old same age not told,
It does add to experience done before,
Want some more, easier this time,
As well as next time perfecting ways,
Confidence displays ordinary similarity,
Naturally considerably confidential,
Privately reserved move on perturbed,
Held in respect different dialect detected,
Away from home dissimilar condone,
Knew putdown was coming bludgeoning,
Condescending remark said for a lark,
Funny for everybody at my expense,
No recompense or recompensed return,
Take it on the chin accept funny laugh,
Agree situation comedy ha-ha move on.

PAINTING NARRATING

Telling a story in a visual language,
Not in a usual descriptive obvious way,
Don't want to be contrived derived applied,
I should only suggest implying design pattern,
My style is abstract colour repetition juxtaposition,
How it reads needs interpreting vaguely not literally,
That's to say I don't always know what I mean,
Until I hit the right chord note be spoken for,
Colour mood attributes conclude true,
A feeling of representing correlation,
Between different parties apart not together,
Harmony or conflict depict reasons to,
Exist out of the ordinary no comradery,
Selfish mood representation bargaining,
Leaving out usual displays of combatting,
Formal conflict opposing sides derides,
Noncompliance as no defiance pretence,
No confidence or diligence only romance,
My heart telling colours apart mood interlude.
Misconstrued as feelings true usually blue.

LOTS OF OPTIONS

Difficult to focus on the day,
My choice is varied and open,
Looking around sun breaks through,
Reflection glaring everything bright,
Optimistic all right don't lose sight,
Focus on single problem at hand,
Can see many more distracting,
Demanding attention recollecting,
At ease wanting to appease all,
Before they get too tall and large,
Tackling previous adventure,
Nomenclature gets me thinking of,
Horticulture setting seed manure,
Greedy feed spring in the air,
Crocus yellow pushing through,
Brown soil mother earth giver of,
Life new birth from the earth,
Seasons cycle springing to life,
Daffodils sign of garish yellow,
Optimistic time has arrived,
Plant out plants use useful.

RHUBARB RHUBARB

I love rhubarb on my breakfast cereal,
It puts a real zing into morning,
Milk wants to separate less great,
Juice and sugar counteract,
Making the syrup join act,
Serial killer joins along,
Keeping it all billabong,
Set up for the day joining fray,
Commissionaire's commission,
Paid not afraid balustrade,
Lean on masquerade,
Covering up blushes,
Got hot rushes,
Gingered up,
A pudding slop,
Delightful team,
Share dream,
Insolvent cream,
Separating glean,
Syrup separates,
Making cream,
Winning team.

NEW YEAR

Starting afresh all seems different,
Don't want to be reminded what's left behind,
Finished with all that dross,
Good chance to start positive,
Change rearrange made plain,
Bold decisions taken makes,
For solving difficulties easily,
Clear mind reminds bind,
Abused parts careless,
Repair or discard old,
Hate waste fold,
Time against fix,
Equation weighs,
Thought through,
Up to you,
New chance,
Make romance,
Half a chance,
I will approach you,
Fantasy fantasise,
Fantastic futuristic.

NEXT IN LINE

For a time combine,
Different words with rhyme,
Avoiding satire lyrical,
Making fun of umbilical,
Closely attached joined,
Forged together,
Whatever the weather,
Sublime rain or shine,
Comforting comfort,
Delusionary convert,
Makes sense now,
Science of solution mix,
Particles combine,
If only for a time,
Long enough to collude,
Without being rude,
Solitude avoid,
Coy annoyed,
Upfront runt,
Nothing to hide,
Along for the ride,
Taking from both sides.

ABOUT TIME

Things are expected to come about,
As a matter of order routine,
Expected delivery on time,
Setup executed each semester,
Taken care of not short,
Order of play no delay,
Time ordered manner,
Direct debit account,
Gets paid automatically,
Less virtual contact the better,
Don't bother sending letter,
No pitter-patter,
On time reminds,
Function functionality,
Punctual delivery,
Late delegates,
Library ticket expires,
Return items,
Back cash back
Cash in,
Insolvent returns,
Accountant alarmed,

Doing no harm,
Time to abandon,
Sinking ship,
Life rafts,
Head up,
Above water,
Sinking feeling,
Watered down,
Cork debulk,
Life ring,
Swimming,
Lifeboat,
Kept afloat,
Lifesaver,
Ship to shore,
SoS alarm,
Tapped out,
Dot dash dot,
All I got,
Brought ashore,
Rig commodore,
Saved life at sea.
Camaraderie.

WINTER APATHY ATTACK

Can't be bothered to do anything,
Everything looks boring dull grey,
Outside inside as well,
As far as I can tell Hell!
My psychology says do something,
Anything start doing not condescending,
Put lights on sod costs,
Driven mad by winter sad,
Trying to remember glad,
Play some music full of cheer,
"Oh dear" horrible repeat,
Other people are happy,
Condescend reprimand,
Ghastly folk bespoke,
Alright for others not me,
Down in the dumps,
Enjoying rude solitude,
Confiscate navigate,
Lost in myself,
Usual wealth of ideas,
Has disappeared,
Commandeered by commander,

Not in command
Around bend,
Desperate disparate,
Illusion confusion,
Wait impatient,
Delay pay,
Not involved,
Self-absolved,
Let off smelly,
Nothing on telly,
Disinterest persists,
Tried making lists,
Someone please insist,
Assert revert,
Leave alone pervert,
Quirk of nature,
Assimilator,
Tributary flows,
Takes away repose,
Inventory disposed,
Acentric eccentric,
Rhyming metric.

APPRECIATE HELP

Got a sympathetic letter understanding problems,
This has cleared my mind bit of a reprimand,
Got into a property pickle being fickle,
Couldn't see a way out plenty of doubt,
Needing advice to make problem nice,
Stuck for ideas thinking in areas,
There must be a solution solve resolve,
Sometimes things just happen,
And they have my case looks bad,
A bit misunderstood if only could,
Trod upon conundrum stepping out,
Leaving no doubt, no clout about,
Apportioning blame framed,
Painted myself into a corner,
Little Jack Horner honing skills,
Playing a game set to remain,
In denial now on trial for pushing,
Too far without permission,
Considering abolishing of,
Honesty tell a lie complied,
Unfortunate deception got,
Away with it again who's to blame?

I've tried to consolidate repudiate,
Translate into accommodation,
With planning regulation,
Allowed guilty not proud,
Didn't mean things to go this way,
Controversy moral discrepancy,
That just happened my way,
I feel apologetic pathetic,
Only help from respected persons,
Can help now in too deep neep,
Tides washing over my feet,
I feel stranded reprimanded,
All at sea being pulled out leaving,
No doubt that I've got it all wrong,
From beginning to now updating,
Affirmative consolatory conservative,
Considerations forthwith without,
Any problem who's shout its mine,
Now I realise deposit repository,
Caused a calamity over ambitious,
My problems are self-inflicted derisory,
Could happen to anybody as well as me.

WRITING THERAPY

Must keep writing to occupy myself,
Utmost importance state of mind,
To be kind to myself keep thinking,
Ideas aren't always obvious,
Just start playing my part,
As if art broadly speaking,
It can be internal problems,
Something heard on radio,
Sparks an opinion to act upon,
Matter of fact or no reason,
Pleasing myself dwelt upon,
Fine now occupied letting,
It flow counteract not detract,
From observed view of new,
Opportunities offered in local,
Vicinity obligatory tasks taken,
Hastens prompt attention to,
Assist with sharing caring,
Not letting good fortune,
Pass me by for being shy,
Wanting to comply with,
Said deficiencies.

CHILLY FOR THE BIRDS

We put out food peanuts for poor hungry,
They're quick to raid plunder the offering,
Sun is out still winter cold life unfolds,
Straight on to it mercy-mercy,
All is forgiven help yourself,
They do in turns happy returns,
Over and over, bullies raid,
Magpie's squirrels crows,
From above below side,
Sinister greedy take from needy,
Little finch crest take turns yearns,
Family of sparrows in turn,
Long tailed tits hospitable bits,
All squabble rationed out,
Fight non left out lots of lots,
Take what they've got to,
Apportioned care concerned,
Fortuitus alive survive,
Back to the nest share contested,
Eat pest bugs tidy up cuddle comfort,
All for one before night sets in dark.

SUBLIMINAL SELF

I had an unusual night's sleep,
I must have been asleep but felt awake,
Dreaming scenarios of good fortune,
Anxieties put to rest solved resolved,
Fantastic good fortune asserted,
Impossible problems sorted,
Delusion confusion simplified,
This all happened on another level,
Waking sleep aware to be fair,
Resolution to act upon awake,
A good lead to proceed needy,
Easy as a dream come clean,
Solved resorted to problematic,
Tragic fanatic fantastic bureaucratic,
Ideas range resorted cavorted,
Vilified impression duration,
Convalesce duress countless times,
Nonetheless mischievous cheeky,
Implied derived contested affected,
Conscience subliminal directive assumed.

INDIRECT EFFECT

Arts way of realising positive change,
Making note of correcting directing,
Expressing saying another way,
By doing so ideas unravel,
Making a different understanding of,
What was first obvious original,
To having an alternative outlook,
Interpretation recollection that other,
People aren't seeing from a different angle,
Representing changes needing to be made,
From my opinion showing another way,
Not literally spelling it out to offering,
Another option suggestion correction,
That bypasses jurisdiction set by,
Authority predominately incorrect,
With the effect of derailing circumspect,
Political misdirected unpopular bias,
Wanting to dominate proceedings,
In a direction not representative of,
The collective retrospective directive,
Creating a revolution of ideas pending.

ALWAYS OPEN

To ideas influenced by life itself,
Must keep busy for sanity,
Doing rueing pursuing can-do,
Got to must do I ask you thank you,
It's all possible venture forth,
North and south open mouth,
Astonished relinquished vacant,
Good ideas kept clear for fear of,
Not replenish kept full admonish,
Repent lose argument dent,
Taken on the chin begin again,
Conflict too direct lost effect,
Change again refrain complain,
Persistent relent argument,
Always different interesting,
Pursuing difference of opinion,
What differs is worthy of note,
Accelerate down open lane,
Want to pertain gain accepted,
Acknowledged perception correctly,
Right idea open mind rewind,
For the love of words absurd.

APART OF IT APART FROM IT

Outsider belongs twixt betwixt,
Wanting to be apart but staying out abstemious,
I feel this way not always sometimes,
Mood prevails off rails then on,
Individual individuality paramount,
Self-assured also lacking in confidence,
Wanting to join in when it suits me,
Trying to find consistency constituted,
Put together made up wanting to join,
The collective society part of a team,
Playing the game set to retain combined,
Paying my fair share of taxes to government,
Choosing using public transport libraries,
Trains roads planes opinions complaints,
Newspapers political sides voting votes,
Writing taking notes practical jokes about,
Politicians' party's places of authority,
Non congeniality theatre football pitches,
Public parks fun larks join in constitution,
Speak out against pollutions keep green,
Apart of it in deep misconstrued rude true.

DURING DURATION

Got to certify certification,
To avoid calamitous calamity,
That regularly regulates relegation,
Dissipating disputes despite dissolution,
Regulating regular customers consuming,
More than their fair share of food going to,
Market marketed remarkably easily due,
Its quality qualifying quality always sells,
What people are looking for to distribute,
Through a distributor distributing at a fair,
Price more than forgiving fortunately,
Fortuitously fortunate frontrunner taking,
Unassailable lead with greed leaving,
Tailenders trailing behind set to remind,
Of famous fortuitus victories to the victor,
Subscribing subscriptions supplement,
Subversive sublimations sufficient as a,
Matter of course of course off course,
The defendant attributes the said supplier,
Will determinedly defend diligently all,
Derisory indeterminate inconsequential,
Deliberations thrown up by the afore said.

CAN BUT TRY

Of course, I will do my best with life's conquest,
Put to the test challenged rearranged,
Working within my means by all means,
Know what I mean averagely to the test,
Replied to all incoming outwardly,
Deciphered hidden meanings supposed,
Sales catch phrases aimed to catch,
Not falling for that spurious try it on,
Straight reply deny understanding,
Pretentious come again?
Extracting relevant facts,
Detect humble humbleness,
Sorry for trying it on obliged to,
As part of finding limits persist,
The conquest manifests itself,
To boldly step out leaving no doubt,
That fresh air will clear my head,
The said is good state of mind,
Clear away bad badness,
Discrepancies lingering,
Holding back new beginnings,
Have to reinvent audacious,

New appraisals to augment,
New ideas to brighten up,
Any old day anyway,
Hither too forth combatting,
Encumbered encumbrances,
Holding me back from advancing,
To a higher level portentously,
Maybe pretentiously fortuitously,
Delivering custom made charade,
To a new stage of deliverance,
Welcomed by friendly friends,
Who tell me not to try too hard,
Feeling lost I agree easy,
Makes me realise I'm low,
Bit below par distant feel,
Tired trying to make life real,
Get with it in tune singing,
Tune in my head la la la,
Looking observing taking in,
Thinking mulling ideas over,
Don't want to waste time,
Wanting the right idea to,
Spring forth to act upon,
It's refreshing to think I have the,
Power to decide. Work or hide,

Face up to facts face it head on,
Break the ice don't procrastinate,
Anymore give time wasters what for,
Now I'm getting around to sound,
Music functional rhythm doing,
Inspired myself to make a start,
When I'm on song singing along,
Bang a gong ding-dong plink plonk,
I know I take ages to get going,
Pursuing doing insidious cantankerous,
At last, don't interrupt in a rush,
Contrary contentious continuous,
Continually concentrated can thus,
I will sure thing got going at last,
Somebody stop me don't get in my way,
All said and done diddle-dum conundrum,
Running along make it on time,
Now I'm late for important appointment,
Can't forgive myself on the shelf,
Who needs money or wealth,
Hidden away with stealth lost,
Fortune can't be presumed,
Must assume lost gone,
No going back move on,
Easier said than done,

For god's sake start,
Stop the hesitancy lark,
Embark on a task,
Don't Park remark,
Keep in the dark,
Only privacy,
Congeniality,
Remember me,
Mister controversy,
Misdemeanours,
Miss spelt delt,
Misappropriate,
Bad case of lose face,
Revenge sought,
Make amends,
Try again,
Balderdash,
Avoid crash,
Make post dash,
Trip over trash,
Spent up no cash,
Never learn return,
Same thing twice,
Ignore advice,
Complicit trice,

Complicated device,
Leave alone condone,
Twice shy deny,
Apply tact,
Who me?
Controversy,
Paternity leave,
Ill conceived,
Who's idea anyway,
Subject subjective,
Personal personalise,
Derive at despise,
Better next time,
Stupid boy,
Allowed it to happen,
Vain train of thoughts,
From within without,
Due care to be fair,
Blind view of you,
Assumed too much,
Carefree let it be,
Similarity comparison,
Evoking rejection,
Not again refrain,
Hurt before adoring,

No more candours,
Resist from list,
Humbled apologist,
Correct this time,
Correctly directly,
In place disgrace,
Improve delude,
Food for thought,
Get head straight,
For every body's sake,
Me as well can tell,
Can but try denying,
Wee wry smile defying,
Compiled trial,
Posing a threat,
Too fine a balance duplicate,
Copy over and out,
Hung over hangover,
Hung up hangovers,
Wild rover all over,
Necessary necessity,
Complicit complicity,
Dysfunctional function,
Displace displaced,
Mouth bad taste,

Evergreen obscene,
Few and far between,
Keep it clean,
Once has been,
Can but try defiled,
Rigmaroles unfolds,
Bought and sold consoled.
Considerate degenerate,
Deflecting attention away,
Complimentary considerately,
Can but try defying.

MAKE SENSE

I'm trying my best but find everything difficult,
Being disabled doubly so,
I don't like being dependant on anybody,
Don't want to put them out,
I need help when it suits me,
Mealtimes cup of coffee,
Medication tablets to be taken,
The timing critical crucial,
Rely on wife matron dependant,
To ask feels like harassment,
My routine is important vital,
Must talk through procedure,
Helps to verify definitely,
Eliminate triviality,
Concur what needs to be done,
Read mail emails act out,
Delegate what can't be done,
Reply deny resort to,
Things fitting into order,
Making sense of recompense,
Polite no arrogance.

AROUND IN CIRCLES

Trying to contact at NHS hospital just didn't happen,
It is too big referral letter sends me back to GP,
Delegated a lot on their shoulders,
Open new folder refresh start again,
Want to complain but refrain blame,
Go back to my dentist resist list,
Persistent contest consistent,
Fresh referral pulls a tooth,
Hospital hospitable suitable,
Spit it out no doubt clout,
Sweet tooth to blame refrain,
New appointment made,
Check-up cheque pays,
Pain no delays rain check,
Told must do ought to,
Regularly regular,
Irrational ration,
Circulars circle,
Circumscription depicts,
Eviction evicts,
Round and around.

KEEP INVENTING

Have confidence in your own ideas,
Let them project forward realistic project,
Think of problems it might create,
Cover all permissions granted not related,
How will it offend drive around bend?
Understand problems comprehend,
Bound to contravene planner's regulations,
Seek prior approval be convivial,
Draw up plans make amends,
All depends on friends comprehend,
Can I afford to act like a lord?
Sensible not absurd ridicule fool,
Thought it through and through can do,
Adapted idea for fear not been clear,
Better now hesitated solved resolved,
Control paramount not restricted afflicted,
Want to be free to do what I've got to do,
Half the battle don't lose rattle acceptable,
Concept freedom detect friends oblige obligatory,
Conform the norm don't blow up a storm calm,
Not repenting my latest invention brand new.

FLOUNDERING

Not sure where I'm at like to think cool cat maybe prat,
Confidence can evaporate in an instant,
Not always resistant to criticism or changes,
I'll take it on the chin then bounce back,
Steadfast as she goes nobody knows,
Best look confident will get me through,
Rest on my laurels beg steal borrow,
It will all work out later or tomorrow,
Confound inconsiderate bigots,
Inflexible hard cases no give up pluck,
Insistent puritanical persistent muckers,
Leave me out to fend for myself,
Abstemious used to it competitive life,
Strife can't rely on do it all for yourself,
Best way to get job done properly,
Make own mistakes rectify faults,
Contrarily have faith in others,
To get jobs done reputations insist,
Good work leads to more taken on,
Life rolls on consider considerate,
Want to relate not a fish out of water.

ENGLISH IDENTITY

I'm not really aware of it as I'm in it,
If I have to it's full English breakfast,
Roast beef and Yorkshire pudding,
Mine's a pint of what's on tap gov,
Are you alright love,
What's natural is understood,
Take my place in the queue in line,
Nobody pushes in a sin,
Got to be fair show despair,
A bit risky comedy of lies,
Got a new motor John?
Shakespeare plays,
Much ado about nothing,
Tempestuous Tempest,
Follow sitcom,
Coronation street,
The square Eastenders,
Chivalrous gentlemen,
Umbrella briefcase,
Pinstripe suit,
Loads of money,
Not being funny.

IMPOSTER SYNDROME

Don't feel worthy or qualified,
To take on and tackle such afore said,
Out of my depth swimming,
Couldn't spell for a toffee,
Now know that isn't important,
With spell checkers correctors,
It put me off furthering a career,
Wish I'd had more confidence to pursue,
Study English at university,
Come to me later in life strife,
It all seems about confidence,
Recompense arrogance pretence,
Boldly head on anything presuming,
Trickster risk taker self-assured,
Conman salesman carry can,
No good carrying it off,
Getting away with it,
Must admit a trick,
Trick of the light,
Making it alright,
Fight or flight.

I CAN'T START UNTIL I'VE HAD A COFFEE

Feel vacant no ambition Monday morning,
Dawning of Aquarius singing in my head,
It will stay for the day now,
Looking aimless waiting for the start gun,
Brought for me it arrives,
Comma in my sentence life's sentence,
The race has begun out of the blocks,
Slightly burnt bitter-sweet,
Cleared brain fog dogging me,
Instant recognition rejuvenation,
Now have ambition reconciliation,
Refreshing uplifting recanting,
Patience has returned patiently waiting,
Planning aims regains,
Addiction satisfied,
All come clear no fear,
Moving on soft connection,
Alert retorts convert,
All to gain now refrain,
Aquarius delirious.

METICULOUS IMPETUOUS

I'm afraid to say this sums up my personality,
I am inpatient want everything yesterday,
In a precise order of delivery, a certain way,
That's my way of doing delivering merchandise,
Contrive in a rush hurry conspiracy afflicted,
Man know thy self I do this is true,
Age has made me slow down a bit,
A perfectionist perfecting peculiarity,
Attention to detail inherent afore said,
Done on time allowing for my confine,
A way of working quickly functionality,
Conscripted depicted plausible laudable,
Done on time remind sublime to an end,
Reputation depends on sound delivery,
Subsidiary of good upbringing homely,
Don't condone left alone thoughtful,
Do my best put to test impertinent,
Prescribed deride can't hide from,
Officious official impetuous meticulously.

NOTHING SPECIFIC

Oceans away from latest controversy,
All at sea with complacency let it be,
Trying to decide along for the ride,
If I wait something will happen,
Sure to evolve out of the blue,
Penny pinching jurisdiction,
Tight delight when right,
Brighten up smiling cup,
Want to know from below,
Feel in charge power large,
Explain regain pertain,
Gift of the gab off the tongue,
Let things lie tell a lie despise,
The way you must sell soul,
To open up opportunity,
That was there all along,
Now going for a song,
Sing it baby bling it,
Shiny contrive alive,
Perchance derive,
Specific chance mine,
Collective my directive.

FINDING MYSELF

Hasn't been straightforward,
Many twists and turns remade learns,
Apologetic concerns forgiveness forgiving,
Conscience clear and muddy,
Has set me on a course of renewal of course,
Improved learned experience experienced,
Doing better this time shaken off confines,
Rules are set to be broken often taken,
Remade revoked presumptuous bloke,
Taken chances lost romances jilted,
Fallen in love out pout nowt pucker up,
Self-confidence bashed crashed panache,
Taken in stride along for the ride tide,
Sink or swim drown play clown trounce,
Pounce upon good idea revered,
Reverently harnessed green credentials,
Offering good credit crediting my account,
On account of creditworthiness bit auspicious,
Dodgy accounting balancing the books as if,
I was a crook hell bent on transcribing,
Decoding double entry rewards in my favour,
A favourable outcome assertive duality myself.

MOUSE TRAP

Had to catch the little chewer,
Anything electric wires it desires,
Plum stones just tidying up,
Crumbs bread a nibble,
Squeeze through entry pursue,
Destiny stopped tempted by cheese,
Fell for the trap done for poor chap,
Similar of mice and men conundrum,
Help to support family only ordinary,
Got in through escape route fenced off,
Mr big keeps out no doubt warm indoors,
Not for his nib's family resident calamity,
Fuss over nothing take little from big boots,
Scaredy cat avoid wanting to play,
Big pause caught out playful trap,
Out of bounds confounds game remain,
Don't see what good I do to imbue,
Tidy up little waste recycle not seen,
Glean morsel small world take from plenty.

MOSS

Atypical cell,
Mimic its base,
Parasitic madua,
Antibacterial molecule,
A poultice on a wound,
Would heal quicker,
Has life regenerating properties,
Mixed with yogurt,
Simulate repair renewal,
Placed on damage,
Pre-history cave dwellers knew,
About its properties,
The power of moss
It absorbs and holds water,
Sponge like,
Soothes broken skin,
Allowing repair,
To begin again,
Back to base level,
Convivial medication.

SUCCESS

I achieved something out of the ordinary,
It gave me a feeling of great achievement!
I wasn't expecting as I was winging it,
Something from memory wishing I'd,
Paid more attention to rectify details,
Contrary contrariness accomplished,
Accomplishments acknowledged,
Set me on the road to achieve more,
Candid candour I applaud plaudits,
Puns made aplenty punctuality,
Bang on time remind reminiscent,
Of humorous conformality commissioned,
Collaborating with consensus concerned,
Deviating from permanent perpetual,
Presence of mind to subliminal kind,
Of intuitive way forward new presentation,
Delivery of old ideas revamped into arbitrary,
Could go anywhere. With no repetition,
Algorithmically a subsidiary substituted,
With an allowance for recompense,
Deliverance of afore said capitulating,
Commandeering trophies victoriously.

FRESH AIR

Awake breathe in a hit,
Oxygen can't compare,
Everything brighter heady,
Ready for anything,
Bring it on begin,
Challenge myself in good health,
Get out cycle get my fill,
Next routine drill,
Move can't keep still,
Happy doing not misconstruing,
My list persists,
Order of play without delay,
Importance reluctance,
Insistent resistant,
Hesitate full-on,
Remark disembark,
Avoid trouble,
At the double,
Singular mind,
Ideas combined,
Partnership relinquished,
Gone to my head,

Bad decision,
Part of a team glean,
Pull together,
Spark off each other,
Two minds better,
To deliver,
Not a quitter,
Good idea,
Made up,
Delighted by,
Clear delivery,
Common decency,
Heard spread word,
Proud to say,
Share compare,
Air voice,
Opinion choice,
Singing loud clear,
Don't disappear,
Want to defer,
Come again,
Spring down,
Country lane.

LET DOWN

Ways of the world are letting me down,
Having trouble fitting in,
I must ask myself do I want to anyway?
Like insurance possibly maybe?
It probably won't so don't,
Covering an abstract probability,
Reality isn't real anymore,
I'm in the wrong game,
Defying complying denying,
Somehow attached to something,
I should really let go of,
Start afresh appraisal dismissible,
Look to a new venture,
Venture forth for what it's worth?
Attachments avoid,
Commitments tying me down,
Freedom desired tired,
Stand tall let go,
Hangers on conundrum,
Insecure freedom,
Attached bureaucrat,
Once cool Cat,

Caught out howzat,
Let team down,
Only a game,
Pertain framed,
All the same harmed,
Alarmed protect,
Version of dialect,
Difference says,
Leaders led,
Away from trouble,
Being let down,
Moribund calamity,
Darkside dominates,
Can't relate or participate,
On a plate castigate,
Put off before wanting more,
Routine upset don't get,
Harassed flipping heck.
Smooth route turned on head,
Which way to turn adjourn,
Solemn sojourn.

IN THE SYSTEM

Apparently, I'm recognised as waiting to be triaged,
Assessed how urgent my case is, I could tell them,
Years wait or ASAP if that's possible admissible,
Admitted to hospital consultant consults importance,
Relevance resembling recognising repudiation,
X ray scanned proof demand assertive,
Wait to hear if all is clear now old dear,
Conclusive isn't illusive only illuding,
Protruding needs extracting benefacting,
Uncomfortable to live with long in the tooth,
Struth Ruth uncomfortable truth undesirable,
Pathetic apologetic sympathy sympathises,
Comprises altruistic all for one conundrum,
But surely its my turn patient patient patiently,
Waiting assessment correlating correctly,
Ready and waiting uncomplicating,
When you are, solve my resolve resolutely,
Politely contritely confess duress painfully.

ARBITRARY AD HOCK

Proposition lacking justification of conviction,
Random anything could happen wayward pretention,
Its probably going to happen anyway so let it,
This way is random no formal appraisal,
Contravening all laws of normality,
Beg to be different not complying,
Supposition to which can't be changed,
Or rearranged obscure collection,
Fitting together abstractly adroitly,
Circumspectly unusual different,
Wanting to relent backward sent,
Argument lost at whose cost?
Refrain never again pertain,
On the wane not the same,
Symbiotic compliments complain.

CLEAR BLUE SKY A BUTE

Drawing me outside must obey the command,
Other things to do defer refer to bin,
Implicit behaviour paramount,
Let other problems go unattended,
Heady fresh air seeing clear,
Solved my resolve in an instant,
Reticent resistance reoccurring,
Retrieving reminiscent of memories,
Held dearly sky clearly flying kite,
Lifting and away pulling holding,
Thrill thrilled thrilling absolutely,
At one with outside don't deride,
Heady air can't compare or dare,
Absorb resolutely resolution,
A beautiful day good for the soul,
A real Bute all mine for the taking.

SHRILL SOUND

Of circular saw cutting through floorboards and my ears,
Banging, and knocking gouging out grout clearing out,
Router deepens groove allowing smooth finish finished,
Drill spills affirmative interlocutor firmly in place,
Conducting wire leaving no trace connected positively,
To correct supply Ac-Dc from solar panels in parallel,
Through E V charger adroitly to connecting point,
Waterproof external plug socket to charge an electric,
Car via solar battery storage and app to show voltage,
Used to top up car storage potential correct potential,
Positively conductively connect ability assuredly,
A safety RMC built in has a neutral cut out if overloaded,
Sounds good to me shrill but in tune all working well.

CHANGED MY MIND

Appreciating what I've got has changed my plot,
Had been thinking about drastic actions,
Complete change seemed attractive,
I had got myself into a panic unnecessarily,
I had to calm down be more positive,
Thinking through all effects who affected,
Whatever I do ties in other people,
Responsible actions considerable considered,
Can't just choose to be wayward tied in,
Restrictions restrict freedom doing,
Should be used to planning by now,
Making any move involves undertow,
Keeping good flow of ideas moving forward,
Problem solving navigating around beyond,
Challenging challenges accomplished,
Change of mind refined absolutely.

STATUTORY SETTINGS

Finally got to a point where I can start,
From the beginning I begin again,
Seems like a country mile leafy lane,
Dappled ruffled baffled kafuffle muffled,
Winding my way around safe and sound,
Being told to get out away from straight,
And narrow take in air to be fair dare,
Easier said than done consider all,
Left to my own device's standards open,
My next step is striding out setting pace,
Not too fast energy to last economy metre,
Whistling tune all mine buying time to rhyme,
Contrary obligatory obligations obsessively,
Upsetting the status quo unbalanced,
Reprimanding reprehension fair wind set fair.

TOUCHY

I sure am careful where you tread explosive,
Handle me with kid gloves carefully,
I'm imploding disrupting disturbing conflicting,
Unstable but still able functioning equivocal trouble,
Limits crossed over and over to the double,
Funny how sanity can unlock insanity,
Root and branch turning over a new leaf,
Conflicting jurisdictions lawlessly judgemental,
Allowing anarchy subjective subliminal to supplement,
My subliminal aspirations tactfully positive jurisdiction,
An affliction I must bear, not by choice or obligation,
But just inflicted affliction self-inflicted jumble of,
Pedantic go-one better judgemental judgements,
Harassing law-abiding anarchists disrupting afore said,
Unequivocally befriending bad taste go ahead punk,
Make my day I will have to say sorry get it right controversy,
Politely touch and go deliver correctly hither say,

NON-DESCRIPT EXPRESSION

I use it to describe something out of reach,
Where is my "Bring Fetching?"!
I know what I mean so does my wife,
By the directive tone of my voice,
My language of choice is discriminatory,
Derogatory expletive condescending foul,
Inarticulate swear I know better to the letter,
I need to listen to myself insult good health,
A wealth of reprimanding misunderstanding,
Once frustration has been dispelled,
Back down to earth adorable lovable,
Black dog has had his say unconscionable,
Defamatory air is blue objective true,
Dispelled condescending repetition,
Frustration consoled concealed satisfied,
Don't deride applied application applicable,
Forsaken fumbling fluctuations formidable.

SUMMER LONG

It seems to keep going,
Not complaining enjoying the warmth,
August 2023 flowers in garden still flowering,
Trees in full leaf grass needs cutting again,
Generic buzz words keep up with trends,
Got to be with it not without yes yes yes,
Climate change has rearranged order of play,
Complex effects much of dependant interplay,
Adapting without realizing naturally,
Cause and effect directly affected,
Now doing what I used to be rueing,
Construed of feeling blue mood true,
A feeling of backend Ish in the air care,
Autumn fall soon to display colour change,
Growth done its job now put down to earth,
Consolidated reinvigorated adapted.

CAUGHT IN LIMBO

Big decisions depending on each other,
Waiting for a call to help decide,
Nothing happening and have left messages,
People are getting back work after holiday,
Back to routine I don't fit in between,
Don't want to push too far being a canvasser,
Wait my turn a lot to learn patience,
Impatiently waiting for a response,
Absence abscond away from desk,
Taken leave problems perceived,
Thoughtful thoughtlessness I digress,
Persistent persistence prevalently,
Purveys predominately promiscuity,
Important digress non the less,
Left out diverted not sure what for.

CAR SALESROOM

Booked appointment but away from desk,
So must look around all on show,
The coffee machine is sales magnet,
Background muzak pretentious allure,
Pep up those who don't want to be there,
Only work there, "seen anything you like?"
Mine already booked old traded in,
Paperwork signed iPad scribbled fingernail,
Code entered password numberplate "E"
Which I'm very proud of front of the Que,
My chance to be "E" obnoxious look at me,
Greener than you, smelly exhaust rear end,
A gifted chance taken new romance,
In love with my fantastic new petrol free,
Faster conscience free elementary must be.

SHOULD I MOVE?

A big decision while I am still able responsible,
I don't really want all the hassle upheaval,
My house is too big so must downsize,
It's served its purpose children now gone,
It would release some of its capitol,
Free up its running costs relieve burden,
I'm not attached to anything can change,
Where do I start, box up possessions to keep,
Now I start thinking about it horded a lot of rubbish,
Must be ruthless only commodities served purpose,
The thought of all this is invigorating bringing on change,
Embracing rearranging maps navigating exciting,
I could explore new ways to live retire defy comply,
Mustn't procrastinate get help delegate,
Psychologically have got too attached to home,
Must embrace for the better change make it happen,
On my shoulders responsible formidable do.

OFF THE HOOF

Unbridled thinking not aloof,
Down to earth for what it's worth,
Down to earth spontaneous,
Humour brought down realistic,
Made a joke of humorously,
Instantaneous bureaucratic instance,
Offering no resistance,
Contentious rigmarole consoled,
Confections admissions asunder,
Pretentious pretentions,
No regulations deviated,
Quickly assimilated,
Behaviour humbled,
Humility humoured,
All sense and purposes,
Deliberately disturbed.

OH! DEAR

Reading the newspaper everything looks dire,
Black and white scuppered my plans,
We're possibly in recession but recovering well,
From pandemic better than other countries,
Optimistic but depressed, up down rates clown,
More fool you me too tardy boo,
Shelve ideas don't sell hold fast won't last,
One thing effects another compounding problems,
Optimism conundrum could be a good time to buy,
Buyers' market risky keep it plain simple frame,
Lose out got no clout laughing matter pitter-patter,
Obvious to see deny me risky belligerent fool,
Careful not to lose out patience needed,
Wait to see nonconformity complies applies,
Don't suffer fools play by rules dissembles.

ADAPTING REACTING

To frustrations protracting growing expanding,
Stubbornly seemingly exponentially experimentally,
A different way of advancing representing old versions,
The same thing but different analogy similar to ones,
Used before dissimilar more ergonomic balanced,
Fitting in with ways being normal expected direct,
Artificial understanding set mathematical path,
Algorithm efficient automatic equation set,
Sets and squares multiplications times over,
Inventive proactive didactive commiserate,
Circulate delegate hand down second hand,
Seen before don't ignore or deplore candour,
Best behaviour separates wrong from right,
Making it contrite alright set to blight fright.

SELECTIVELY SELECT

A selection of ideas to pursue concurrently,
My current thinking is the value or worth,
Of undertaking certain goals and benefits,
And doing so are they worth entering,
Should they be ditched along with other,
Bright ideas with no hope of success,
I must quantify their return in terms,
Not just monetary value but satisfaction,
The return is assessed as complicit with,
What I would expect from minimum layout,
Small growing to a worthy profit gain,
A friendship previously taken onboard,
Not appreciated at first then realising,
Its significance surprisingly returning,
A hearty undervalued friendship.

QUICK CHANGE

Change of plan be a man rearrange,
Think quickly adapt to different stage,
Turn page over act with certainty,
Don't allow negativity positively,
Presumptuous prompts politely,
Adapt adaptations deftly,
Get into new groove assertively,
Commander for fear of losing,
Winning not abusing rings true,
Left losers behind kind,
Reprimands reminiscent concurrently,
Contravene collate conventions,
Resolve resolutely inherently,
Brought about correct reflection,
No recollection aberration,
Correct effect defect.

STICKY WICKET

New bifold doors cause a problem hinging,
Each section depending on the next to run true,
When one doesn't line up it throws the others out,
Such is life when you depend on others to act correctly.
Individuality is expected as we're all different,
Getting in tune with a collective is tactical,
The art is to understand demand applicable,
Depending on needs unforeseen clean glean,
Selfish isn't compatible with partnerships,
Dependency compatriot competition,
Friendly collaboration lawful deviation,
Input collective suiting all sides dependant,
Swerve away from true line wicked spin,
Bereft from playing the game deviation.

THINKING OF OTHERS

What they should be doing as I see it,
Without intruding tactfully suggesting,
Have you ever thought about?
Dangling a carrot gold thought,
It is very cathartic but not nosey,
Use humour to infiltrate the said!
If they haven't thought of it already,
Sometimes coming from somebody else,
Makes them think plausible possible,
A helping hand oblige defy comply,
Talents supressed pass conquest,
Yes, clicks into place join the race,
Why don't I defy sense purpose,
Have a go not below above it all,
All said and done conundrum,
I'm in the know you know!
Privileged benefactor benefiting,
Passing the buck without,
Running amuck caput,
Do or die death defy,
Life isn't easy appease me,
Troop along trolleying,

Be a man dead pan,
Confucius say confusingly,
Philosophically have a go,
Nothing to lose loosely,
Only certain certainty,
Loss of face no disgrace,
Commonplaces embarrass,
Harras hassled ruffled,
Kerfuffle nonbattle,
Spittle bucket kicked,
Slop soaks away,
Nonother less hither say,
Controversy affirmative,
Deliberation deliberately,
Assessed nonconsensual,
Senseless consent,
For the sake of argument,
Sensible syllable,
Derives complicitly derides,
Confides friends,
Stop around bend,
Saves safely,
Complicit anthology,
Jurisdiction manifests,
Implicitly personally,

Nosey parker my business,
Unequivocal equally,
Shared out portions,
One for you one me,
Won't go hungry,
Dum-diddle-de-dee.

UNPRODUCTIVE

Much of life has no purpose,
Seem to be doing as a matter of course,
Routine driving my has been in between,
Selection selective no directive directly,
Constructive construction misconstrued,
Feel used borrowed leave alone old Tone,
Press on get jobs done finally finished,
Cleared away clearly wiped clean,
Smells fresher freshly start afresh,
Production produces prevarication,
Put off had enough repetitive stuff,
Leave alone public liability insured,
Against representable angst,
Finally finish fortuitously forgiven,
With a produced production produced.

Author Anthony P Prior,
disabled with MS.

www.ingramcontent.com/pod-product-compliance
Lightning Source LLC
Chambersburg PA
CBHW071455080526
44587CB00014B/2114
9781805414452